In the Footsteps of Explorers

Francisco Pizarro

Journeys through Peru and South America

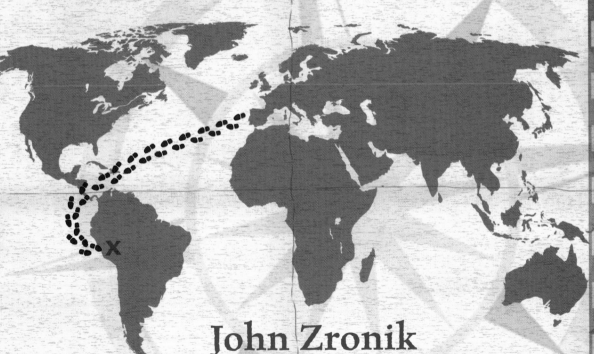

John Zronik

Crabtree Publishing Company

www.crabtreebooks.com

Crabtree Publishing Company

www.crabtreebooks.com

For Charlotte

Series editor: Carrie Gleason
Coordinating editor: Ellen Rodger
Editors: Rachel Eagen, Adrianna Morganelli
Design and production coordinator: Rosie Gowsell
Cover design and production assistance: Samara Parent
Art direction: Rob MacGregor
Scanning technician: Arlene Arch-Wilson
Photo research: Allison Napier

Photo Credits: The Art Archive / Biblioteca d'Ajuda Lisbon / Dagli
Orti: cover; Art Archive / Museo del Oro Bogota / Dagli Orti: p. 5;
Bettmann / Corbis: p. 15; Gianni Orti / Corbis: p. 26; Jacques Jangoux /
Photo Researchers, Inc.: p. 10 (bottom); Steve Kaufman / Corbis: p. 20;
Bildarchiv Pressischer Kulterbesitz / Art Resource, NY: p. 11, p. 22;
Charles & Josette Lenars / Corbis: p. 31; Michael Lustbader / Photo
Researchers Inc.: p. 12; Mary Evans Picture Library / Photo Researchers,
Inc.: p. 17 (bottom); Tom McHugh / Photo Researchers Inc.: p. 16;
North Wind / North Wind Picture Archives: p. 8, p. 9, p. 10 (top),
pp. 12-13, p. 19, p. 23, p. 24, p. 25, p. 29; David Parker / Photo
Researchers, Inc: p. 17 (top); Scala / Art Resources, NY: p. 5;

Snark / Art Resources, NY: p. 27; Spanish School / Museo del Ejercito
Madrid, Spain / Bridgeman Art Library: p. 14; other images from stock
photo cd

Illustrations: Lauren Fast: p. 4, p. 6 (top); Roman Goforth: p. 9; David
Wysotski, Allure Illustrations: pp.16-17

Cartography: Jim Chernishenko: title page, p. 10, p. 22

Cover: A painting of Francisco Pizarro murdering the Inca
leader, Atahuallpa.

Title page: Francisco Pizarro's voyages took him from Spain, across the
Atlantic Ocean, through the Caribbean, and on to the Pacific coast of
South America.

Sidebar icon: The conquistadors were lured to America by reports of
gold, such as this South American native gold artifact.

Crabtree Publishing Company

www.crabtreebooks.com   1-800-387-7650

Cataloging-in-Publication Data
Zronik, John Paul, 1972-
    Francisco Pizarro : journeys through Peru and South America / written by John Zronik.
       p. cm. -- (In the footsteps of explorers)
    Includes index.
    ISBN-13: 978-0-7787-2411-7 (rlb)
    ISBN-10: 0-7787-2411-5 (rlb)
    ISBN-13: 978-0-7787-2447-6 (pbk)
    ISBN-10: 0-7787-2447-6 (pbk)
    1. Pizarro, Francisco, ca. 1475-1541--Travel--Juvenile literature. 2. Incas--Juvenile
literature. 3. Explorers--Peru--Biography--Juvenile literature. 4. Explorers--Spain--
Biography--Juvenile literature. 5. Peru--History--Conquest, 1522-1548--Juvenile literature.
6. South America--Description and travel--Juvenile literature. I. Title. II. Series.
    F3442.P776Z76 2005
    985'.02'092--dc22
                                              2005001086
                                                   LC

**Published in
the United States**
PMB 16A
350 Fifth Ave.
Suite 3308
New York, NY
10118

**Published
in Canada**
616 Welland Ave.
St. Catharines
Ontario, Canada
L2M 5V6

**Published in the
United Kingdom**
73 Lime Walk
Headington
Oxford
0X3 7AD
United Kingdom

**Published
in Australia**
386 Mt. Alexander Rd.
Ascot Vale (Melbourne)
V1C 3032

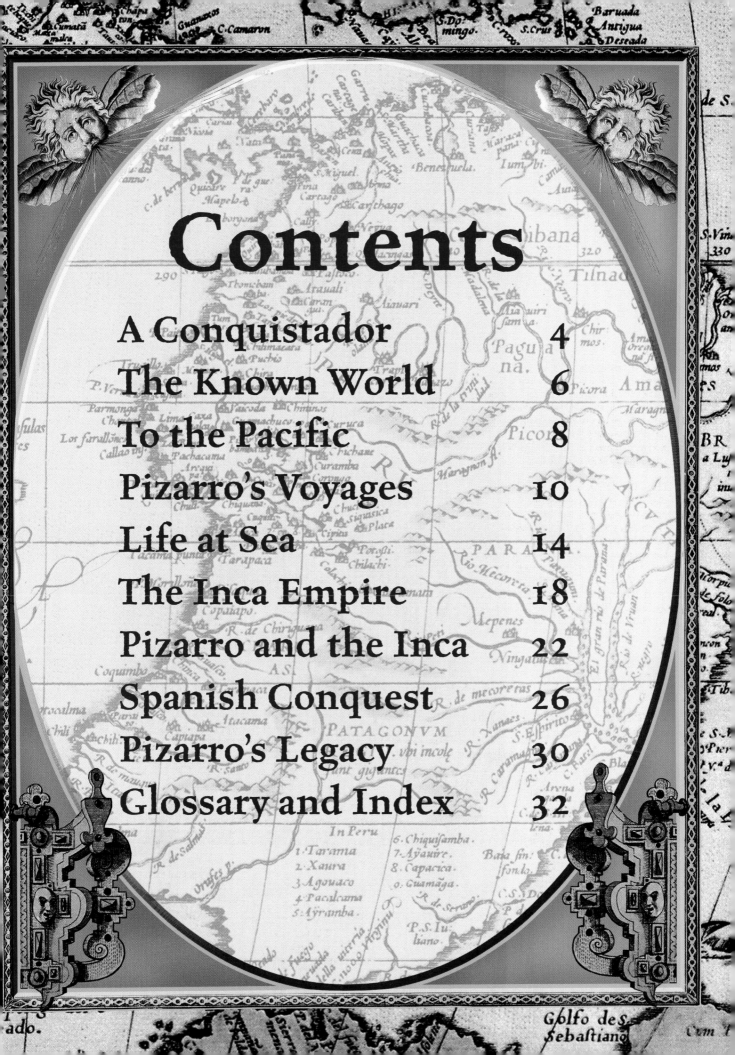

Contents

A Conquistador

Francisco Pizarro was a Spanish conquistador, or conqueror. His journeys took him across the Atlantic Ocean, through tropical jungles, and over the mountains and coastal deserts of South America. Pizarro's expeditions sowed the roots for the Spanish conquest of Peru.

An Explorer is Born

Francisco Pizarro was born in Spain. As a teenager, he joined the military, but failed to rise in rank. In 1502, Pizarro left Spain and sailed to Hispaniola, an island in the Caribbean where the Spanish had set up a colony. He later helped set up a new Spanish colony in Panama, where he grew wealthy as a farmer and part-owner of a gold mine.

The Conquistadors

The conquistadors were mostly men from Spain who went to the New World to try and gain wealth and positions of power. By discovering new land, the conquistadors could appeal to the Spanish king for permission to rule over it, and the people living there.

(above) Francisco Pizarro led the first Spanish expedition down the Pacific coast of South America.

In the Words of. . .

Pizarro needed to find gold to be used as a source of currency, and natives to be used as **allies** and as workers to set up a new colony in Peru. One of the ships on Pizarro's second journey down the Pacific coast of South America came across a native raft carrying gold and other precious metals.

"[On the raft were] many pieces of silver and gold as personal ornaments... including crowns, belts and bracelets, armor for the legs and breastplates; tweezers and rattles and strings and clusters of beads and rubies...They were carrying many wool and cotton mantles and tunics...and other pieces of clothing colored with crimson, blue, and yellow."

(below) Legends of a South American kingdom made of gold inspired many conquistadors to explore the continent.

- 1475 -

Pizarro born in Spain.

- 1502 -

Pizarro leaves Spain for Hispaniola.

- 1541 -

Pizarro killed in Peru.

The Known World

- 1492 -

Christopher Columbus (above) was born in Genoa, in what would become Italy. Under the flag of the Spanish king and queen, he crossed the Atlantic Ocean and landed on an island of the Bahamas chain. After his voyage, many other Europeans came to the New World.

In the Middle Ages in Europe, people did not know much of the world beyond their borders. Many believed that by sailing west across the Atlantic Ocean, they could reach Asia. Instead, they found the New World.

The Age of Exploration

Around 1500, countries in Europe, including what would become Spain, began to send explorers to the New World to set up colonies.

(above) Europeans wanted to reach Asia because they wanted spices, silk, and other Asian trade goods.

(left) Explorers were surprised to find the American continents blocked their westward route to Asia. This old map shows the coastline of North and South America as it looked to explorers. They did not know what lay in the interior.

Reconquista and Religion

King Ferdinand and Queen Isabella united two powerful kingdoms of the Iberian Peninsula, in what is now Spain. Together, the king and queen fought to retake Spanish territory that was ruled by the **Moors**. This is called the Reconquista. During the Reconquista, the king and queen made contracts with military leaders who were granted power to rule, under the monarchy, over the lands and peoples they conquered. An important part of the contract was that the conquerors claim the territory under the Christian religion.

(right) Christians follow the teachings of Jesus Christ, who they believe is the son of God. Christ was thought to have died on a cross for people's sins.

Merchants and Conquerors

Port cities of the Iberian peninsula prospered through trade with one another and by acquiring goods through explorations of the African coast. Spanish merchant companies were set up that had a main investor who stayed at home and funded the company, and a partner who did the traveling, buying, and selling. These companies set up trading posts in the lands they discovered, where they ruled over a native work force and controlled the resources of an area.

(left) Religion played an important part in the Reconquista. Christianity was the only religion allowed. Priests often went with conquistadors to convert the natives to Christianity. The queen wanted everyone in her empire to be Christian.

To the Pacific

On an expedition captained by a conquistador named Vasco Nunez de Balboa, Pizarro became one of the first Europeans to see the Pacific Ocean from America.

(left) Conquistador Alonzo de Ojeda captured a native leader, Caonabo, after a settlement in the Caribbean was destroyed by natives. Caonabo later died in a shipwreck on the way to Spain. Ojeda shared a similar fate.

Problems at San Sebastian

Pizarro joined an expedition led by Alonzo de Ojeda to set up a new colony on the South American mainland. The colony, San Sebastian, was attacked by natives, who waited outside the settlement's walls with poisoned arrows.

Of the 300 men who set out from the nearby Caribbean island colony of **Hispaniola**, 200 died from native attacks, illnesses, and starvation.

Help from Encsico

Ojeda abandoned San Sebastian and left Pizarro in charge. Back in Hispaniola, explorer Martin Fernandez de Encisco set sail for San Sebastian with two ships full of supplies. When Encisco arrived, Pizarro and his men were hungry and ill.

(background) Many of the settlers at San Sebastian died from tropical diseases that they caught in the jungles. The Spanish had no immunity, or natural defenses, to fight these diseases. The Spanish also introduced European diseases to the native peoples.

A New Leader

The survivors of San Sebastian left to set up a new colony at Darien, in what is now Panama. A native village existed there and the Spanish battled the natives and took over the village. The settlers at Darien **revolted** against Encisco's leadership. Vasco Nunez de Balboa, a stowaway on one of Encisco's ships, was chosen as the new leader. Pizarro and Balboa became friends.

South Sea Adventure

Balboa made contact with the native peoples around Darien. Some welcomed and exchanged gifts with the Spanish, while others fought them. The leader of one native group told Balboa of a route to the Pacific Ocean, and of the **Inca**, and their vast amount of gold. Balboa led 190 men on a journey across the **isthmus** of Panama to find the Pacific Ocean with Pizarro as second in command.

(left) On September 29, 1513, Balboa claimed the Pacific Ocean in the name of the king and queen of Spain. He called it the South Sea.

- 1508 -

Settlement at San Sebastian founded, the first on the South American mainland.

- 1519 -

Conquistador Hernán Cortes (above) sets the foundation for the Spanish conquest of Mexico.

- 1522 -

Pizarro hears reports of native peoples with gold and silver.

Pizarro's Voyages

Pizarro formed a partnership with Diego de Almagro, a fellow Spanish conquistador, and a Catholic priest named Hernando de Luque. Inspired by rumors of a rich native empire to the South, Pizarro and his partners planned a voyage down the Pacific coast of South America.

Down the Coast

Pizarro set out down the coast with a crew of 80 men and four horses. The crew ran short on food and picked and ate unripe and bitter fruit to survive. Many of Pizarro's men died on the voyage, including five killed in battles with natives. The mission eventually returned home, having only made it just past the isthmus of Panama.

(top right) In a fight with natives, Almagro lost sight in one of his eyes after it was pierced by a spear.

PANAMA

Tumbez

PERU

SOUTH AMERICA

Lima

Pizarro's Voyages:

First Voyage →→→

Second Voyage →→

(above) Pizarro's first voyage ended in failure. After being plagued by insects in the mangrove swamps of the coast, they were forced to return home.

A Second Journey

On Pizarro's next voyage, he took 160 men aboard two ships. Almagro led the crew on one of the ships, Pizarro on the other. They decided that more men and supplies were needed to continue the expedition. Almagro took one ship and samples of gold back to Panama to encourage men to join them. A man named Ruiz sailed the second ship south down the coast to see what lay ahead. Pizarro and his men set up camp near the San Juan River, in present-day Colombia, to await their return.

Contact

Ruiz and his crew encountered a **balsa** trading raft laden with Inca goods. When the natives saw the Spanish ship coming, many jumped overboard to get away. Three natives were captured by Ruiz to be trained as language interpreters. Language interpreters were important to conquistadors because they enabled them to communicate with natives. The explorers needed information from the natives about the land, the people, and how to get food. Ruiz returned to Pizarro at his camp with the prisoners, and the goods carried on the raft.

(above) Pizarro and his partners sign an agreement to share in the riches of South America's Pacific coast.

An Unexpected Obstacle

When Almagro arrived back in Panama, he learned that the new **governor** did not support Pizarro's expedition. The governor ordered that any of Pizarro's men who wanted to return to Panama would be rescued. When Pizarro heard this, he drew a line in the sand and asked the men willing to continue in his service to step over it.

Venturing Onward

The expedition continued and Pizarro's men discovered the Inca city of Tumbez, which is in the north of present-day Peru. In Tumbez, the natives welcomed the Spanish. They served the Spaniards meals on gold and silver plates. The Spaniards saw **temples** full of gold and silver decorations. Native leaders gave Pizarro and his men many gifts when they left Tumbez to return to Panama.

(above) Pizarro and his crew were stranded on an island off the coast of Colombia for seven months. They survived by eating snakes and shellfish.

- 1524 -
Pizarro's first voyage departs from Panama.

- 1526 -
Pizarro joins in a partnership with Diego de Almagro and Hernando de Luque.

- 1526 to 1527 -
Pizarro's second voyage down the coast of South America.

Help From the Crown

Despite Pizarro's discovery of Tumbez and its riches, the governor of Panama still refused to support his expedition. In frustration, Pizarro traveled to Spain and presented the king and queen with golden objects and told of his South American adventures. Eager for more gold, the king and queen agreed to support Pizarro, giving him the power to rule any territory he discovered.

(background) According to one report, Pizarro drew a line in the sand and said: "On that side lies the part which represents death, hardship, hunger, nakedness, and abandonment; this side here represents comfort. Here you return to Panama - to be poor! There you may go on to Peru - to be rich. You choose what best becomes you as brave Spaniards." Thirteen of Pizarro's men chose to stay with him.

Navigation in the 1500s.

- Celestial Navigation-

Judging the ship's position based on the sun or the stars (above) is called celestial navigation.

- Dead Reckoning -

To calculate a ship's position, the speed, time, and direction, as well as how much the ship may have drifted, was taken into account.

Life at Sea

Pizarro and his men had few navigational charts for their voyages, but, thanks to the reports of earlier conquistadors, such as Cortes and Columbus, they knew what supplies to bring, and what to expect of the native peoples.

Pizarro's Fleet

Historians believe that Pizarro's ships were caravels. The caravel was a light ship used between the 1400s and 1700s. Caravels had two or three **masts** with square and triangular sails. The design of the caravel's sails made it easier to maneuver than other ships. It was also easier to navigate in shallow waters because it was smaller than most ships.

(below) Pizarro's ship flew his own flag, which was awarded to him by the king of Spain.

Men and Cargo

Pizarro's ships carried men, horses, and supplies, and there was a specific place for each of them onboard. Casks of flour, wine, food, and weapons, including **crossbows**, **hatchets**, and guns, were kept below deck in the ship's hull, or body. The ship's crew also slept below deck. There were few comforts - a hammock offered the most luxury a crew member experienced.

(left) A drawing of a Spanish caravel from the 1500s.

Duties of the Crew

Each man onboard had specific duties. The ship's captain was in command, and made sure crew members did their jobs. Ship's boys were responsible for keeping track of time, leading morning prayers, scrubbing decks, and serving hot meals. A ship's surgeon cared for the ill and injured. Food was in limited supply, so each man was given a daily ration, or portion. Higher ranking officers received more or better food than lower ranking men.

(below) Rats and cockroaches often made their way into ships' food supplies.

Chuno

On their South American voyages, Pizarro and his men complemented their food supplies with native food sources, such as potatoes and corn. They also discovered methods the Inca used to preserve foods. The Inca used a type of freeze-drying to preserve potatoes, which created a food called chuno.

1. Spread thinly sliced potatoes on a cookie sheet and place in the freezer overnight.

2. Remove from freezer and mash into a pulp.

3. Allow to dry out all day.

4. Repeat the process day and night for a week.

5. Your chuno is now good for a year.

(below) Crew members' meals included salted meat, bread, fish, and cheese.

(background) Explorers used different types of ships for their journeys in the 1500s. What was common aboard all ships was that life at sea was not easy. The crew faced challenges such as low food supplies, cramped quarters, bad weather, and illness. Tempers often flared and fights broke out. The success of a voyage depended, in part, on how well a captain controlled his crew.

(below, right) An hourglass filled with sand was used to keep time on ships. It took 30 minutes to empty one end and then was turned by the ship's boy.

(below) Many crew members became sick with scurvy, a common disease at sea caused by a lack of vitamin C, which is found in fresh fruit and vegetables.

- Finding Latitude -

To determine a ship's position, explorers need to find their latitude, or position north or south of the equator.

Astrolabes (above) and quadrants (below) were both used to measure latitude. One arm of the instrument was aligned with the horizon and the other with the sun or stars. The greater the angle, the further from the equator the ship lay.

The Inca Empire

The Inca were the most powerful South American native group when the Spanish arrived. They had conquered other native peoples and incorporated them into a vast empire that covered what is now southern Ecuador, all of Peru and Bolivia, and part of Chile.

Center of the Empire

According to one Inca legend, their first leader, Manco Capac, was born from the sun. He established the empire with his sister, Mama Ocllo, who the Inca called Daughter of the Moon.

The sun presented Manco Capac with a golden rod and told him that if the rod was placed into the ground and disappeared, then that land was the place for the Inca to live. That place was the city of Cuzco.

(background) The Inca lived in the valleys of the Andes Mountains, the mountain chain that runs along the coast of South America. The high mountains sheltered their towns and cities. Machu Picchu, shown here, was not found by the conquistadors, and remained hidden until 1911, nearly 400 years after the Spanish arrived in South America.

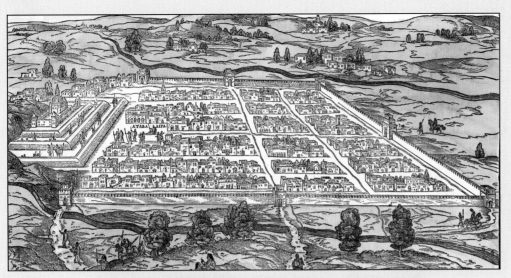

(left) The city of Cuzco was at the center of the Inca empire. This illustration of the city is from after the Spanish took it over.

(right) According to Inca legend, Manco Capac taught the men how to farm, while Mama Ocllo taught the women how to weave, cook, and look after a home.

-1100s-

The Inca settle
in Cuzco.

- 1438 -

Inca empire
starts to grow,
conquering
other native
groups.

- 1525 -

Inca leader
Huayna Capac
dies of smallpox,
a disease
introduced by
the Spanish.

- 1525 -

Inca civil war.

(above) The Inca grew food, such as corn and potatoes, on terraces cut into the mountainsides.

(above) Most Inca lived in small homes with walls made of mud brick or stone. Roofs were *thatched* using thick grass.

(left) Nobles wore headdresses with feathers from colorful birds from east of the Andes. The forest of the Amazon basin was the border of Inca territory.

The Sapa Inca

Huayna Capac was the Sapa Inca, or Inca emperor, around the time Pizarro first arrived in South America. The Sapa Inca kept strict control over the lives of the natives they conquered. Some welcomed the Inca, others resisted. Huayna Capac was in the north of his empire battling natives in Ecuador when news of the death of members of his Inca royal family from disease reached him. The Inca empire had an efficient communication system across the empire. Well-built roads ran through their lands on which runners, called *chasqui*, delivered messages.

A Divided Empire

It was not long before disease also killed Huayna Capac and his **heir**. Two of his sons, Huascar and Atahuallpa, fought each other for control of the empire in a bloody **civil war**. Huascar had been made ruler, but Atahuallpa controlled the Inca army. With the power of military might behind him, Atahuallpa won the war and became the ruler. Huascar became his brother's prisoner, but still had many loyal supporters.

(left) Llamas and alpacas were important livestock. Llamas were used to carry heavy loads and their wool was used for clothing.

Pizarro and the Inca

Pizarro returned from a visit to Spain in 1530 as an adelantado, or licensed conqueror. This meant that he had royal permission, based on the information about the Inca empire he had gathered and presented to the king and queen, to rule over Peru.

A Tough Journey

The start of Pizarro's third journey at sea was slowed by strong winds, so he decided to travel overland instead. Their voyage on land was not any easier. Some of Pizarro's men died in the unmapped jungles, on frozen **glaciers**, and while marching through deserts on their way to find the Inca.

(below) When Pizarro reached Tumbez on his third voyage, he found the city destroyed. Pizarro learned of the Inca civil war and knew to use it to his advantage.

PANAMA

SOUTH AMERICA

Tumbez

Cajamarca

PERU

Lima

Cuzco

Pizarro's Third Voyage

Strategic Advantage

An empire weakened by being loyal to different leaders could be conquered easier than a united empire. Pizarro quickly set about making alliances with natives loyal to the defeated Inca, Huascar.

Journey to the Inca

Pizarro set out to meet Atahuallpa at the Inca city of Cajamarca after natives told him that the Inca army was camped there. On the way, Pizarro and his men had to cross the Andes Mountains. As they approached Cajamarca, they saw thousands of Inca soldiers camped outside the city.

(above) On their way to the Inca ruler, Pizarro and his men passed Inca watchtowers, but were allowed easy passage.

(left) Pizarro led his horse through the difficult and narrow passes of the Andes Mountains.

- December 27, 1530 -

Pizarro departs on his third voyage.

- November 16, 1932 -

Inca ruler Atahuallpa captured.

- August 29, 1533 -

Atahuallpa assassinated.

Abandoned City, Swift Battle

Pizarro and his men were allowed to enter the city, which was nearly empty following a battle between Huascar and Atahuallpa's armies. After taking up position in the town square, Pizarro sent a small group of men to meet the Inca leader camped outside Cajamarca. At the meeting, it was agreed that Atahuallpa and Pizarro would meet the following day.

Just before nightfall the next day, Atahuallpa and 5,000 to 6,000 Inca entered the town square where Pizarro and his men had been waiting.

Slaughter of the Inca

The Inca leader told the Spaniards they had no right to attack and rob his people, pointing out the brutality with which the Spanish had treated the natives since entering the land of the Inca. The Spanish announced their intent to take over the Inca's land and convert them all to Christianity. A fight broke out, and the natives were slaughtered. Pizarro and his men fought their way to Atahuallpa's throne and captured the Inca leader.

(background) Atahuallpa was carried into the square atop a golden throne called an usno. According to journal entries later made by both Inca and the Spanish, the Spanish tried to intimidate the Inca with their horses, animals the Inca had never seen before. Intimidation was a tactic that conquistadors used against native peoples.

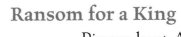

Ransom for a King

Pizarro kept Atahuallpa as his prisoner. In an effort to secure his freedom, Atahuallpa told Pizarro he would give him a room filled with gold and another with silver. Pizarro agreed to free the Inca leader if he kept his word. Atahuallpa gave Pizarro the gold and silver. The loot was divided among Pizarro and his men, with the largest share kept by Pizarro.

(left) The Spanish and their allies were greatly outnumbered by the Inca. Conquistadors sometimes fought with guns called harquebuses, but mostly with steel swords.

Atahuallpa's end

The Spaniards betrayed Atahuallpa, sentencing him to death. The Inca leader was to be burned at the stake, but Atahuallpa was told if he became a Christian he would be hung instead. The Inca leader agreed, and was given the Christian name Juan de Atahuallpa before he was killed.

(right) Friar Vincente Valverde pressured the Inca leader to convert to Christianity and save his soul, and his body, from being burned.

Spanish Conquest

After the battle at Cajamarca, Pizarro quickly marched on to Cuzco, and took the Inca capital. The years following Pizarro's battle at Cajamarca mark the beginning of the Spanish conquest of Peru.

Inca Revolt

After the murder of Atahuallpa, Pizarro crowned Manco, another Inca **noble**, as Sapa Inca. Pizarro had hoped to control the new Sapa Inca, but horrified by the way the Spanish were treating the Inca people and their greed for gold, Manco organized a revolt against the Spanish. Thousands of Inca marched on the city of Cuzco, but were defeated by the Spanish.

Inca Nobles

Some members of the large Inca royal family were executed by the Spanish. Others were allowed to continue to rule. Many noble women were forced into marriage with the conquistadors. Pizarro himself took an Inca wife named Ines Yupangui, whose name he changed to Pizpita.

During the Inca revolt, the Spanish brutalized the native population, torturing Inca and sending their mutilated bodies back to the Sapa Inca. The Spanish hoped that this would stop the revolt.

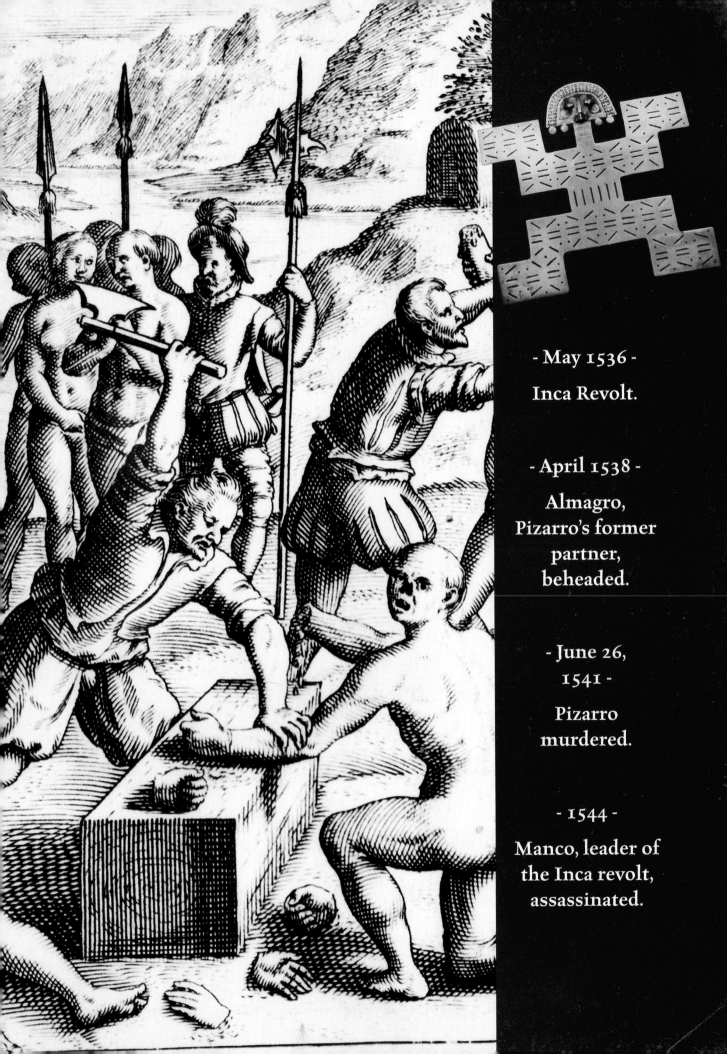

- May 1536 -
Inca Revolt.

- April 1538 -
Almagro,
Pizarro's former
partner,
beheaded.

- June 26,
1541 -
Pizarro
murdered.

- 1544 -
Manco, leader of
the Inca revolt,
assassinated.

Spanish Power Struggle

Pizarro's partner, Almagro, felt his share of the riches was unfair. Pizarro paid for a journey for him to explore down the coast of Chile, where it was rumored there was even more gold. When he returned, Almagro and his men also attacked Cuzco. Pizarro gave Almagro two choices: give up the city or fight for it. Almagro fought, but Pizarro's forces won and Almagro was **executed** in a public beheading.

Diseases and Protection

Even before Pizarro's arrival in the Inca empire, many native peoples were dying from European diseases. When the Spanish settlers, who came to Peru from Panama after hearing of Pizarro's find, started to lose their labor force, measures were taken to keep the natives alive. In some areas, Inca life continued much as it had before the Spanish arrived, in others, such as Cuzco, life changed drastically. The natives were also forced to pay a tribute, or tax, to their new Spanish rulers.

Gold and Slaves

Gold and silver taken from Inca temples was melted down and shaped into gold bars. The gold was used to finance, or pay for, Pizarro's voyages and to set up the Spanish colony. Some of the gold was sent back to the Spanish king and queen. Natives were forced to work as slaves in gold and silver mines, or were enslaved on large farms.

(right) Few gold artifacts from South America's native peoples remain because many were melted down.

(background) Almagro's followers, in return for the beheading, overran Pizarro's palace in the city he had set up on the coast, Lima. Pizarro, who was eating dinner at the time, put up a strong fight, but was badly outnumbered and killed. He was 66 years old.

Pizarro's Legacy

Today, Francisco Pizarro is remembered as one of the great conquistadors in the Spanish conquest of South America. Pizarro's voyages shaped the history and culture of modern Peru.

Inca Way of Life

As more Spaniards moved to Peru, many Inca temples and cities were destroyed and replaced by Spanish churches and cities. Over time, the Inca way of life slowly changed to incorporate Spanish dress, food, and religion. The Spanish also introduced diseases to the Inca that they had no way of fighting. As a result, the Inca population gradually declined.

(right) Today, some Inca descendants still live in the valleys of the Andes.

(below) Pizarro's tomb is located in Lima, the capital city of Peru. Lima was founded in 1535 by Pizarro.

CAPITAN GENERAL
DON FRANCISCO PIZARRO

Probanzas and the Spanish Conquest

The role of the conquistadors in the Spanish conquest of Central and South America is debated by historians today. The main sources of information about the conquest are first-hand reports written by the conquistadors and their men, which were sent back to the Spanish king. These reports, called probanzas, were written to prove to the king that the conqueror deserved rewards, such as titles and pensions, for their work. Some historians today question the facts presented by the conquistadors in these reports, and the role that individuals played in the conquest. The information on events and people in this book are based on the probanzas and some historians' interpretations of these reports.

Artwork

There were no cameras or video recording equipment during the Spanish conquest. The artwork in this book was created later by artists who were not present at the events. For this reason, the events may not have happened exactly as they appear in this book, but in styles that were popular during an artist's lifetime.

Glossary

ally A person or groups who help one another, especially during war

balsa Soft, lightweight wood from a tropical tree

basin The land that is drained by a river and the streams that flow into it

civil war A war between two groups within one country or culture

colony A territory governed by a distant country

conqueror Those that take over a people or country by force

convert To change one's religion, faith, or beliefs

crossbows A type of weapon used to shoot arrows

descendant A person who can trace his or her family roots to a certain family group

empire One political unit that occupies a large region of land and is governed by one ruler

execute To put to death

glaciers A huge river of ice that flows down from mountains

governor An official who governs, or oversees, a territory

hatchet A small, short handled axe

heir Someone who inherits land, money, or a position of power from another person

Hispaniola A Caribbean island now home to the countries of Haiti and the Dominican Republic

Inca A South American native royal family that established an empire along the Andes

isthmus A narrow strip of land between two larger masses of land

mangrove A tropical tree that forms dense thickets along tidal shores

masts Vertical poles that support sails on a ship

Middle Ages The period in European history from about 500 A.D. to 1500 in which Europe was broken up into smaller kingdoms

Moors Muslims, or followers of Islam, from North Africa. Islam is a religion based on the teachings of Allah and his prophet Muhammad

mutilate To damage by cutting, tearing, or removing a part

New World The name given to North, Central, and South America by Europeans after they discovered that the continents existed

nobles Members of the most powerful or wealthy group in a society

preserve To keep food from rotting

priest A person who leads or performs religious ceremonies

revolt To rebel or try to overthrow

Spanish conquest The period in history in which the Spanish introduced their way of life to the New World

temple A building used for religious services

thatched Straw or grass woven to make a roof

Index

1 2 3 4 5 6 7 8 9 0 Printed in the U.S.A. 4 3 2 1 0 9 8 7 6 5